Jamie Victoria Barnes

fantastic ideas for
forest school

FEATHERSTONE

FEATHERSTONE
Bloomsbury Publishing Plc
50 Bedford Square, London, WC1B 3DP, UK

BLOOMSBURY, FEATHERSTONE and the Feather logo are trademarks of Bloomsbury Publishing Plc

First published in Great Britain 2020 by Bloomsbury Publishing Plc

A catalogue record for this book is available from the British Library

ISBN: PB: 978-1-4729-7372-6; ePDF: 978-1-4729-7373-3

2 4 6 8 10 9 7 5 3

Series design: Lynda Murray

Printed and bound by Ashford Colour Press Ltd

MIX
Paper from
responsible sources
FSC® C011748

To find out more about our authors and books visit www.bloomsbury.com and sign up for our newsletters

Acknowledgements

I would like to thank Logan Gray for taking the beautiful photographs for this book and Nevill Road
Infant School for allowing the use of the school grounds.

Contents

Introduction

What is Forest School?

Forest School is an ethos; it gives adults and children the opportunity to connect or re-connect with the world around us in its natural state. It gives us the space and freedom away from time pressures, technology and everyday life stresses to reflect on ourselves in our most basic forms.

Being outdoors enables exploration, discovery and understanding, not only of the visible natural world and its resources, but also of ourselves on an emotional and psychological level. It allows us to find our inner confidence and the connections between ourselves – both physically and emotionally.

Forest School is a continuous long-term programme that offers us the opportunity to be reflective, to make mistakes and connections, and to have balance within our everyday lives.

Forest School can be anywhere outside, so no matter how big or small your outdoor area is, you can deliver quality activities with the help of this book. The activities are open to interpretation – use them however best they fit in your outdoor environment.

The main aim of the book

Being outside offers young children endless opportunities for playing and exploring which facilitates their learning and development. Young children need to have daily quality outdoor experiences that offer them the opportunity to move their bodies and use their energy. They learn best when they are moving and especially when they are able to explore and be creative, away from the confines of an indoor space. These activities support all types of learners and offer everyone the opportunity to shine and enjoy learning in a relaxed and open-ended way.

This book will give those who are new to and to those more experienced in Forest School and nature pedagogy the opportunity to learn about activities that are centred around the natural world. The outdoor environment enables children and adults to reconnect with nature, which has a profound impact on all development areas including emotional wellbeing. Forest School takes children back to basics; it removes fixed toys and objects and opens up a world full of discovery and unlimited potential. It is incredible what you can create out of a few leaves and sticks…

The ideas in this book will help you to discover and appreciate the outside environment in its natural state as we only need simple resources to create meaningful and rich play opportunities. They focus on the whole child holistically, to support all areas of development and learning, while engaging their creative spirit, independence and self-confidence. You will be amazed at how much children thrive in the natural environment and the positive impact it has on their play, creativity and in terms of overall development too.

Natural resources can be used in many creative ways and these activities will help you build your own confidence in delivering outdoor Forest School sessions in a simple, yet effective, way. Children learn best when they are engaged and having fun – which is exactly what these activities aim to do.

Let's talk safety

Some of the activities require children to work with tools. This will require one-to-one support for each child.

Here are some general rules to follow:

- Ensure that you complete risk assessments that are in line with your policies and procedures to keep children safe at all times.

- Always wear a glove on your non-dominant hand when using tools, ensuring that you are safe distance from anyone else and that there is a first aid kit close by.

- Children must be supervised at all times and must go through a safety procedure when using any tools so that they clearly understand how to use them properly.

- Any tools must be kept in a designated toolkit area that is clearly marked.

- Children should always have access to drinking water while outside.

The structure of the book

Before you start any activity, read through everything on the page so you are familiar with the whole activity and what you might need to plan in advance. The pages are all organised in the same way.

What you need lists the resources required for the activity. These are likely to be readily available in most settings or can be bought or made easily.

What to do tells you step by step what you need to do to complete the activity.

The **Health & Safety** tips are often obvious, but safety can't be overstressed. In many cases there are no specific hazards involved in completing the activity, and your usual health and safety measures should be enough. In others there are particular issues to be noted and addressed.

Top tips give a brief word of advice or helpful tip that could make all the difference to the experience of the activity for you and your children.

What's in it for the children? tells you (and others) briefly how the suggested activities contribute to learning.

Finally, **Taking it forward** gives ideas for additional activities on the same theme, or for developing the activity further. These will be particularly useful for things that have gone especially well or where children show a real interest. In many cases they use the same resources, and in every case they have been designed to extend learning and broaden the children's experiences.

Magical tree spirits

Experimenting with textures

What you need:

- Soil or air-drying clay
- A bowl for each child or pair (if using soil)
- Water in a large container
- A selection of cups for the children to transfer water
- Wooden spoon for each child or pair
- Sticks, leaves, pebbles, flowers or any natural embellishments – be creative!

What's in it for the children?

Children use their senses to explore their surroundings, gathering resources and finding out more about the world around them. They are able to use their inner creativity to design their own tree spirit, as there is no right or wrong way. Fine motor skills are supported in shaping and forming their magical tree spirits, alongside messy sensory play.

Taking it forward

- Create a magical woodland story based around the tree spirits who protect the natural area. Take photographs to create a picture book.

What to do:

1. Decide if you would like to use clay or soil to create your magical tree spirits.

2. If using soil from the ground, encourage the children to place five handfuls into a bowl (more if they want to create a larger tree spirit).

3. Support the children in slowly adding water to the mixture.

4. Encourage the children to use their hands or a wooden spoon to stir until they get firm mud: a sticky dough-like mixture.

5. If you decide to use clay, children can tear off a handful for each of their tree spirits. The size of each tree spirit is individual so the children can use as much or as little as they like.

6. Using a flat surface or their hands, encourage the children to roll their mud/clay into a ball and then flatten it to form an oval shape.

7. Ask the children to find a tree and pat the mud/clay onto the trunk, pressing down the edges so that it sticks, to create their tree spirits.

8. Allow the children to explore the area to collect their natural embellishments and to create a face or pattern on their tree spirits.

9. Can the children describe how they created their tree spirit and what or who it is?

Nature mandalas
Creating patterns with nature

What you need:

- Images of a nature mandala
- Sticks
- Leaves
- Pebbles
- Flowers
- Any natural embellishments – be creative!

What to do:

1. Show the children an image of a nature mandala, explaining that to create one we start from the middle and work our way out.
2. Encourage the children to explore the outdoor area to find and gather resources for their mandalas (individually or in a group).
3. Using soil or a pavement/patio area as the canvas, show the children how to clear a space on the ground with their feet, removing any leaf litter to create a space.
4. Invite the children to work in pairs and to begin by creating a small circular pattern with a chosen resource and share design ideas with each other.
5. They should continue building bigger circular patterns around the initial one until they have created their very own natural art mandalas.
6. Invite the children to look at each other's work and explain how they designed their own mandala.

What's in it for the children?

Children can explore patterns, shapes and textures to create their own unique design, while connecting with nature and discovering natural resources. Teamwork plays an important role in bringing this activity together, through sharing ideas and creating a design.

Taking it forward

- Capture the moment with a photograph and create a natural art scrapbook to reflect on the process of creating a nature mandala.

Capture a moment
Use nature to create a scene

What you need:

- Four sticks of similar lengths
- Leaves
- Stones
- Flowers
- Twigs
- Any natural embellishments – be creative!

Top tip

This activity can be done individually or in groups to support teamwork and communication.

What's in it for the children?

Natural art enables children to be creative while using their senses; it allows them to become familiar with using nature to create new ideas and supports imaginative skills and discovery about the natural world.

Taking it forward

- Take photographs and add them to a natural art scrapbook to reflect on and review the activity.
- Encourage the children to count, measure and compare the sizes of their collected items to develop their mathematical skills.

What to do:

1. Using soil or a pavement/patio area as the canvas, show the children how to clear a space on the ground with their feet, removing any leaf litter to create a space for their scenery pictures.

2. Ask the children to find four sticks of similar length and place them on the ground in a square or rectangular shape. This will be their frame.

3. Encourage the children to decide on a picture to create. This could be the view in front of them, the woodlands, flowers; it can be anything that they choose.

4. Invite the children to gather the natural resources they need and place them in view to begin creating their scenery picture.

5. The children will need to use trial and error to see what works and gather further resources should they need them.

6. Support the children by asking questions about their picture and any details they may need to focus on.

Self-portraits
Supporting self-awareness

What you need:

- Mirror for each child
- Leaves
- Stones
- Flowers
- Twigs
- Any natural embellishments – be creative!
- Tree stump (optional)

What's in it for the children?

This activity allows children to learn about themselves and their bodies, such as facial features. They are then able to make connections with nature as they gather and search for the shapes and textures needed to create their portraits. They can explore what makes each of us unique and individual in our physical appearances.

Taking it forward

- Take photographs of the portraits and of the child so that they can compare and reflect on both.

What to do:

1. Start by giving each child a mirror and ask them to look at their reflection. Encourage the children to point out each of their features and what they are used for. Also talk about colours, for example, eyes, hair and skin.

2. Invite the children to gather natural resources that they would like to use to create their own self-portraits, thinking about the shapes, textures and colours discussed.

3. Using soil or a pavement/patio area as the canvas, show the children how to clear a space on the ground with their feet, removing any leaf litter to create a space. Alternatively, you can use a tree stump.

4. Encourage the children to keep looking in the mirror as they build their portrait, picking out their features, so they do not miss anything.

5. Gather the children together and visit each portrait. Ask the group if they can work out which portrait belongs to which child.

Leaf animals

Exploring nature's wildlife

What you need:

- Selection of animal pictures
- Leaves
- Stones
- Flowers
- Twigs
- Any natural embellishments – be creative!
- Camera

What to do:

1. Show the children some pictures of different animals and ask them to choose any animal that they would like to create using natural resources.
2. Encourage the children to think about the shapes they may need for their animal and invite them to explore and gather their natural resources.
3. Using soil or a pavement/patio area as the canvas, show the children how to clear the ground with their feet, removing any leaf litter to create a space.
4. Support the children to piece the resources together, experimenting with textures to form the basic outline of their animal.
5. Once the children have their basic animal shape, invite them to search for more resources to add features like eyes, tails, wings, etc.
6. Invite the children to show each other the animals they have created and explain why they chose that animal.
7. Encourage the children to take photographs of their natural animal art so they can share with others.

Top tip ⭐

Children may need support to begin with but allow them to make mistakes and use trial and error – it will help build their self-confidence!

What's in it for the children?

The children are able to explore their surroundings, gathering resources and finding out more about the world around them. They are able to use their inner creativity to create their own natural art animal, as there is no right or wrong way. Their fine motor skills will be used as this activity will require hand-eye coordination and a steady hand, especially when adding features and using small fiddly resources.

Taking it forward

- Use photographs of the natural art animals to create a picture collage or an animal storybook for your classroom.

- Encourage the children to create a scene for their animals using more natural resources by showing them the animals in their natural habitats.

- Try this activity during different seasons to see the differences in resources available, e.g. the colours of leaves.

Mud kitchen

Design and build your unique mud kitchen

What you need:

- Paper
- Pencils for each child
- Logs
- Tree stumps
- Planks of wood
- Wooden crates
- Saucepans/cauldrons
- Wooden spoons
- Mud
- Water
- Any natural resources you can find

What to do:

1. With the children, design what they would like their mud kitchen to look like. What features will it have? It could be as simple as two tree stumps with a wide plank of wood over the top as the work surface.

2. Encourage the children to draw their ideas on paper.

3. Bring the children together in a group and allow them to take turns sharing their ideas for the mud kitchen with each other.

4. When you have decided on a design as a group, you can begin building the area together.

5. Once constructed, invite the children to add mud and other natural resources to their new muddy kitchen.

Top tip

- This is a great activity to support teamwork, sharing and social communication.

- Sometimes when it comes to resources, less is more! Some of the best mud kitchens I have seen just use logs, cauldrons and wooden spoons.

What's in it for the children?

Involving the children in the process of building their mud kitchen area will engage them in the activity, making it more meaningful to them. Once the mud kitchen is built, it offers opportunities for imaginative play, sensory play, social communication, construction and design as well as learning about nature.

Taking it forward

- Don't forget that it does not just have to be a mud kitchen – perhaps you can turn it into a mud café or a mud art gallery?

Mud cake bakery
Messy sensory play

What you need:

- Soil
- Bowl for each child or pair
- Water in a large container
- Spoon for each child
- Cake cases
- Petals
- Stones
- Leaves
- Natural embellishments
- Tray to display cupcakes
- Camera

What to do:

1. Ask the children to scoop handfuls of soil into their bowl.

2. Next ask them to add small drops of water to the soil to turn it into a thick mud mixture. Too much water will make it runny and the mud will not stick – encourage the children to experiment.

3. Using their hands or a spoon, help the children to transfer the mud from the bowl into the cake cases.

4. Allow the children to forage for some natural resources to decorate their mud cakes. They could use petals, stones or leaves, for example.

5. Put the mud cakes on a tray and 'serve'.

6. Compare mud cake designs and take photographs.

Top tip

To make mud play dough, add plain flour to the soil and water mixture.

What's in it for the children?

Children are able to experiment with the mud mixture, using trial and error to get the right consistency and using creativity to decorate their cakes. This activity enables the children to play and get messy as they engage in sensory play.

Taking it forward

- Create a mud kitchen café to serve mud cakes, mud pies and maybe even a mud pizza.
- Create a menu for their mud café so guests know what to order.

 Health & Safety

These mud cakes are for play, not to eat!

Going on a bear hunt

Bringing stories to life outside

What you need:

- *We're Going on a Bear Hunt* by Michael Rosen and Helen Oxenbury
- A soft teddy bear
- Logs or materials to build a den (a tent for example)

Top tip ⭐

Be enthusiastic when reading the story to really bring it to life and include the children on the journey.

What's in it for the children?

This idea brings together literacy, gross motor and communication skills. The children are able to immerse themselves in the story, using movement and body awareness to bring it to life. They also have to use construction skills to create the den.

Taking it forward

- Make a natural art picture of a bear.
- Use the story to create outdoor sensory activities with the elements used in the book: water, mud, grass and snow.

What to do:

1. Gather the children outside and read *We're Going on a Bear Hunt* by Michael Rosen and Helen Oxenbury to them.

2. Assist the children in building a den out of logs or resources you may have to hand to create a 'bear cave'. Place the cuddly toy inside the cave.

3. Go on an adventure acting out the story as you go along. This could be in the woods or garden area.

4. Over-exaggerate the movements needed for the story making it a physical and interactive activity.

5. End the story at the cave you have built... but watch out for the bear!

Woodland shops
Introducing mathematics and nature

What you need:

- A work surface (this could be a bench or tree stump for example)
- Leaves
- Sticks
- Conkers or acorns
- Natural resources
- Stones (for money)
- A container for each child
- Chalk to share

What to do:

1. Invite the children to help set up an area for a role play shop. You can use any surface, e.g. a tree stump.

2. Encourage the children to collect natural resources including leaves, conkers and sticks, and to group them by item.

3. Ask the children to collect stones in their container to act as money.

4. Let the children take turns to write up the prices of the items being sold in the shop using chalk.

5. Once the shop has been set up, encourage the children to begin role playing.

6. Use mathematical language and ask questions to further enrich their play and learning experiences.

What's in it for the children?

This is a fun activity that supports communication and language skills as well as mathematical development. It is a great opportunity to encourage counting and the use of mathematical language.

Taking it forward

- You can develop more than one 'shop', so that the children can take it in turns to visit different woodland stores.

- Use this activity at the same time as the mud cake bakery (see page 13) to create more than one role play activity at a time.

Potions laboratory
Making magical woodland potions

What you need:

- Two tree stumps of a similar height
- A wide sheet of wood
- Tuff tray (optional)
- A selection of pots and pans to share
- Spoons to share
- Bucket of water
- Measuring jugs
- Paper
- Pens
- Leaves
- Petals
- Natural resources
- Edible glitter
- Spray bottles
- Watering cans
- Plants

What to do:

1. Place two tree stumps on the ground and add a sheet of wood on top to create a worktable. Alternatively, you can use a tuff tray.

2. Encourage the children to organise their resources in the potions laboratory by placing pots and pans, spoons and any other utensils onto the worktable.

3. Create a designated area for a bucket of water. Ask the children to measure out quantities of water with measuring jugs and to carry the water over to the worktable without spilling any.

4. Next, create an ingredients list to give to the children or write one together with them. Don't forget to add quantities!

5. Assist the children in foraging around the area to collect the resources needed for your potions laboratory, checking that they have collected all items on the ingredients list.

6. Begin exploring and mixing the resources and water together with the spoons to make magical potions.

7. Show the children how to spray some edible glitter onto the final mixture to bring the magic to life.

8. Fill spray bottles or watering cans with the magic potion and ask the children to water any plants that you have in your setting to infuse them with magic!

 Top tip ⭐

Using edible glitter does not harm the environment.

What's in it for the children?

This activity encourages imaginative and magical play that allows the children to follow their own direction of play. You will be amazed at the engagement and role play ideas that they will create with this initial lead in. The children also have the opportunity to develop their literacy and mathematical skills as they create their ingredients lists and measure out quantities, as well as their gross and fine motor skills as they transport water from one place to another.

Taking it forward

- Create a magical story to go alongside the children's role play, e.g. the Woodland Wizard has been captured by a dragon and the only way to save him is with the magical potion...

- Encourage mathematical language throughout, e.g. ask 'How many sticks do we need?', 'How many sticks have you got?'.

- Support literacy and mark making skills by asking the children to write down their ingredients or seeing if they can recognise any letters on the lists.

Forest School TV

Supporting role play and communication skills

What you need:

- Safety goggles and gloves for yourself
- A large, old picture frame
- Two pieces of rope of the same length
- Two trees or branches that are close together
- Gloves for the children
- A small block of wood
- Sandpaper
- Felt-tip pens

What to do:

1. Wearing safety goggles and gloves, remove any glass or hooks from a large, old picture frame.

2. Take a piece of rope and tie one end around the top right edge of the frame. Tie a second piece of rope around the top left edge.

3. Find two trees or large branches that are close together and hang the frame between them, tying the rope securely with granny knots.

4. Ensure that the children are wearing gloves and invite them to take turns in sanding down a small block of wood using sandpaper.

5. Once done, ask the children to draw buttons on the block of wood using felt-tip pens to make it look like a TV remote control.

6. Allow the children to take it in turns to stand behind the frame and entertain the other children – their TV viewers – by role playing, singing and dancing. The possibilities are endless!

What's in it for the children?

This activity presents opportunities for imaginative role play, social interaction, storytelling and communication through performance.

Taking it forward

- Ask the children to narrate and re-enact a well-known story behind the TV.

- Create a woodland documentary on topics learnt outside as a reflection tool.

✚ Health & Safety

Ensure the picture frame is suitable for use before letting the children play with it. Wear gloves and safety goggles to remove any hooks, glass and nails and dispose of them safely. The children should also wear gloves when using sandpaper on wood.

The magic box

Igniting imaginations

What you need:

- A box
- A handwritten letter
- Various small items, e.g. a trinket

Top tip ⭐

You can buy plain wooden boxes that your children can decorate first – this way the magic box will be even more special.

What's in it for the children?

This activity is a great way to support children's learning through play. This initial lead in will allow them to then continue the play following their own direction as their curiosity is ignited.

Taking it forward

- Create a unique story about the magic box. At circle time, begin a story about the box and then ask each child in turn to add a sentence or two.

What to do:

1. You can use the magic box however you wish, but first you must introduce it to the children.

2. Start by saying, 'Every so often something new and magical will appear in the box. If you find the magic box, you must wait for an adult to open it to discover the magic inside. If you touch the box, the magic will disappear!'

3. Write a handwritten letter from a fairy, pixie or dragon or follow the children's current interests.

4. Give the children a task to complete or an initial role play lead in. Some examples are:

   - Place a letter from some woodland fairies whose village was blown away in a storm in the magic box. The letter should ask if the children can help rebuild the fairy village.

   - Hide a black button and a letter from Santa in the magic box. Can the children work out who the button belongs to?

   - Hide some 'lost' gems from a crown belonging to a woodland wizard in the magic box and include a letter asking if the children can make a new crown for the wizard.

5. Place the magic box outside for the children to stumble across. Ignite their imaginations with this play and see where it takes them!

Story stones

Supporting storytelling

What you need:

- Selection of stones in various shapes and sizes
- Warm, soapy water
- Towel
- Acrylic paints
- Paint palettes
- Paintbrushes for each child
- Aprons
- Spray sealer and facemask (adult use only)

What's in it for the children?

Literacy, language and communication skills are supported and developed through the use of the story stones that act as visual aids. Story stones are also useful for exploring rich language as well as the structure of stories.

Taking it forward

- Use the story stones to recall events.
- Create life cycle story stones.

✚ Health & Safety

Always wash your hands after using acrylic paints. Make sure you wear a facemask when using the spray sealer and keep the spray well away from your face.

What to do:

1. Ask the children to collect stones of various shapes and sizes in the outdoor environment.

2. Let them wash the stones in warm, soapy water to remove any dirt and pat the stones dry with a towel.

3. You can either:
   - Paint the stones with characters and items for the children to use to create their own stories.
   - Paint the stones with specific characters or specific items from a storybook to use during story time.
   - Allow the children to select colours and design their own stones using just their imagination and creativity.

4. Once painted, let the stones dry and then finish them with a spray sealer to prevent damage to the paint work. The spray sealer should only be used by the adult and should be kept away from the children at all times. Use the stones to aid storytelling for either made-up or well-known stories.

5. If the children painted their own stones, encourage them to explain what they have designed and to create a story if they would like to. Encourage them to follow the structure of a story and include a beginning, middle and end.

BBQ leaf kebabs

Campfire role play

What you need:

- Eight or more sticks of a similar length
- Moss
- Leaf litter
- Leaves in different shapes and colours
- Thin sticks for each child

Top tip ⭐

The thinner the sticks are, the easier it is to thread the leaves for the kebabs.

What to do:

1. Show the children how to clear a space on the ground with their feet, removing any leaf litter to create a space.

2. Help the children to collect a pile of eight or more sticks of similar lengths.

3. Using four sticks, demonstrate how to make a square on the ground where you cleared a space. This will be the 'campfire' area.

4. Create a tepee shape in the centre of the square using four more sticks so that the structure resembles a campfire.

5. Invite the children to collect moss, leaf litter and various leaves in different shapes and colours.

6. Ask the children to sprinkle moss and yellow leaves over the tepee of sticks to look like flames.

7. Next, assist the children in threading their chosen coloured leaves onto a thin stick to create a leaf kebab.

8. 'Cook' the leaf kebabs over the campfire and sing campfire songs!

What's in it for the children?

This activity develops fine motor control, as the children put the pretend campfire together and thread the leaves onto the stick.

Taking it forward

- Create leaf patterns for the children to follow when threading their leaves, e.g. green, yellow, red.

- Create a role play game around the activity, e.g. cowboys and cowgirls camping in the woods.

Fairy homes

Design and construct homes for small world play

What you need:

- Two 'Y' shaped sticks of similar lengths
- One long stick
- Eight sticks or less – depending on the size of the build
- Moss
- Leaves (bracken is great)
- Stones and any other natural resources you would like
- Fairies or small world toys

What to do:

1. Show the children what a 'Y' shaped stick looks like and ask them to find two 'Y' shaped sticks in the area.

2. Help the children to push the tail end of both sticks a few centimetres into the ground. The further apart the two sticks are, the bigger the house will be.

3. Show the children a longer stick and ask them to find one in the area.

4. Ask the children to place the longer stick across the 'Y' sticks. The long stick should sit comfortably in the 'Y' to act as the start of a roof. This is now the frame of the fairy home.

5. Next, ask the children to collect around eight sticks of roughly the same length. Show the children how to create a wall for the fairy home by taking the sticks and balancing each one diagonally against the long stick, creating a wall at the back of the fairy home.

6. Explain to the children that the fairy home needs to be waterproof. What could they use to cover up any gaps?

7. Encourage the children to search for moss and leaves and carefully place them over the wall and top of the fairy home.

8. Allow the children to be creative in designing their own fairy homes. They can use stones or other natural resources to decorate, perhaps creating a pathway to the front door or a garden wall. The possibilities are endless!

9. Once they have finished decorating, the fairy home is ready to play with. Use some small world toys to support their role play.

What's in it for the children?

This activity helps to improve children's construction skills and encourages them to follow basic instructions to build the structure of their fairy homes. They also have to be creative when designing and building the homes. Once built, the children are able to play together and use their imaginations to create role play scenarios.

Taking it forward

- The children can construct more buildings to go with their fairy homes to create a fairy village.

- Create other small world play structures using the same technique.

Top tip ⭐

The children could tie a piece of string between two sticks to make a washing line for their fairy home.

Stick man

Bringing stories to life outside

What you need:

- *Stick Man* by Julia Donaldson and Axel Scheffler
- One stick per child
- Potato peeler
- Gardening gloves for yourself and the children
- Felt-tip pens

What's in it for the children?

Using literacy and communication skills, the children are able to immerse themselves in the story and use movement to bring it to life. This activity also supports the development of fine and gross motor skills as the children create their own stick men using whittling techniques.

Taking it forward

- Build a woodland home for the stick man.
- Create the stick man's family too.
- Take photographs of your outside journey to make your own stick man picture book.

✚ Health & Safety

See page 5 for tips on safety when using tools.

What to do:

1. Gather the children outside and read to them *Stick Man* by Julia Donaldson and Axel Scheffler.
2. Ask the children to go in search of a stick to be their own 'stick man'.
3. Ensure that you have a clear space around you and that there are no children close enough to get hurt. You should be 'two arms and a tool's length' away from any children.
4. Demonstrate to the children how to hold the potato peeler correctly.
5. Kneel on the floor with one leg raised. Wearing a gardening glove to protect yourself, hold the stick in your non-dominant hand.
6. Hold the peeler in your dominant hand and peel away some of the stick, in gentle movements away from your body. Carefully whittle away a small amount of the stick to create a flat surface to draw on the stick man's face.
7. Do this with the children one-to-one in order keep everyone safe. Let them use the peeler if appropriate, and ensure that they wear gardening gloves.
8. Using the felt-tip pens, let the children draw a face on their stick man.
9. Read and act out the story in the woodlands or garden with the children's stick men.

Three billy goats gruff

Bringing stories to life outside

What you need:

- *The Three Billy Goats Gruff* by Paul Galdone
- **Tree stumps**
- **Plank of wood**

What to do:

1. Gather the children outside and read the story to them.

2. Invite the children to discuss what you might need in order to recreate the story, e.g. you could build a bridge using tree stumps and a plank of wood.

3. Be creative and use what you have to hand, e.g. if you have a pond or a bridge nearby, base the story around the setting.

4. Take turns acting out the story, inviting the children to trot over the bridge or take on the role of the troll.

What's in it for the children?

The children are able to immerse themselves in the story using movement to bring it to life and building the 'set' which, in turn, develops their literacy, communication and gross motor skills.

Taking it forward

- Create a new ending for the story and act it out.
- Build a raft for the billy goats to escape from the troll.

Health & Safety

Always be cautious near water and complete a risk assessment. Be vigilant with the children and explain the safety rules. Risk-taking is essential for learning and development but you must ensure safety at all times.

Wildflower woodland crowns

Creating props for role play

What you need:

- **Thin bendy twigs (willow is great if it is to hand)**
- **Sticky tape**
- **Scissors**
- **Grass blades**
- **Wildflowers**
- **Leaves**
- **Feathers**
- **Natural embellishments**

Top tip

- The children will most likely need one-to-one support with the first stage of this activity as it is quite fiddly and more than two hands are needed.

- Spring and summer are great times of year for this activity if you want to use a variety of different wildflowers.

What's in it for the children?

The children are able to use their fine motor skills to weave their crowns together, as well as creativity and personal preferences to make choices on how to decorate them. They are also able to develop their communication and listening skills as they work with adults or friends to make the base of the crown.

Taking it forward

- Create a story based around woodland crowns: who do they belong to? Do they protect the woodlands?

- Take photographs of the crowns to add to a nature scrapbook.

What to do:

1. Ask the children to search for thin bendy twigs outside. It is a good idea to have collected some yourself beforehand.

2. Next, ask the children to choose two bendy twigs and help them one-to-one to interlock the twigs and make a thicker band.

3. Wrap the band around the child's head to make a crown shape and measure how big it needs to be.

4. Once you have the circular shape, continue interlocking the ends of the additional twigs to create the crown.

5. Use sticky tape to secure the crown. You may not need to use much if the winding of the twigs has worked well and they are interlocked together.

6. Invite the children to search for blades of grass which they can then weave around the crown to add colour.

7. Next ask the children to explore the area and look for wildflowers, leaves, feathers and other natural embellishments to decorate their woodland crown and style it however they wish.

8. The children can then enjoy and role play with their new woodland crowns.

Nature wings

Fairy wings, dragon wings, whatever you decide!

What you need:

- Two arm-length sticks
- A ball of twine or wool
- A selection of ribbon
- Wildflowers
- String
- Any natural embellishments – be creative!

Top tip ⭐

A clove hitch knot and square lashing are great to use to tie your sticks together securely. A guide is available online at www.thechildcareguru.co.uk or you can watch a video tutorial at www.youtube.com/watch?v=9wpb9dELsa8.

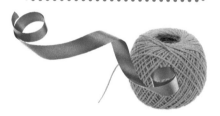

What's in it for the children?

This is an opportunity to explore natural resources and use fine motor skills to tie knots and decorate the fairy wings.

Taking it forward

- Children can use their nature wings to engage in role play and build on their creativity and social communication.
- The children can use paints to further decorate their wings.
- Create a fairy tale story to go alongside this craft making.

What to do:

1. Ask the children to find two sticks that are each the length of one arm.

2. Once they have found their sticks, ask them to use them to make a 'x' shape on the ground.

3. Help the children tie the sticks together where they join at the centre of the 'x', holding them tight and securing the sticks with twine or wool.

4. Show the children how to use ribbons to connect the ends of the sticks together and create triangle-shaped wings.

5. Invite the children to decorate their wings with wild flowers, wool and string – they can be as creative as they wish!

6. Add twine 'straps' so the children can wear their wings during their play.

Woodland shield

Nothing is more powerful than a shield made from nature

What you need:

- Three sticks of similar widths and length
- Twine
- Scissors
- Assortment of coloured wool
- Leaves
- Grass
- Wildflowers
- Feathers
- Bark
- Natural embellishments

Top tip ★

The children will need one-to-one support in order to put together their shield as it requires more than two hands. Alternatively, they can work in pairs.

What's in it for the children?

This activity is an opportunity to explore natural resources and use fine motor skills to tie knots and weave designs into woodland shields. This is a collaborative activity and relies on teamwork and communication to put the shield together.

Taking it forward

- Create a role play game involving the woodland shields.
- Use different numbers of sticks to create different-shaped shields, following the same pattern.
- Use this activity alongside other activities in this book, such as nature wings (page 27) to create a bigger role play theme.

What to do:

1. First, ask the children to find three sticks of similar widths and lengths. Once they have found their sticks, invite them to place them on the ground in a triangular shape.

2. Help the children cut three long pieces of twine using the scissors and tie each point of the triangle together securely to create a shield. The best way to do this is to use a clove hitch knot followed by square lashing (a guide is available online at www.thechildcareguru.co.uk or you can watch a video tutorial at www.youtube.com/watch?v=9wpb9dELsa8).

3. Take the ball of coloured wool, tie the loose end to a corner on the inside of the shield. Help the children to tightly wrap the wool in the same direction around the shield. To keep this tight, loop the string twice around each end of the stick as you wrap.

4. Once the children have wrapped the twine around the shield in one direction, ask them to use the scissors to cut the wool from the ball and tie in a double knot.

5. They now need to repeat steps 3 and 4 in another direction, pulling tight, to create small squares.

6. Explain to the children that now they have created a pattern on their shield they are able to go foraging for their natural resources: leaves, grass, wildflowers, feathers, bark – anything that they wish to use!

7. Demonstrate to the children how to weave their resources through the wool to create patterns and decorate their unique shield.

8. Once the children have finished decorating their shields, they are ready to be played with, e.g. using the shields to fight off a woodland dragon.

Magic wands

Sprinkle some magic around outside

What you need:

- One stick for each child
- Different coloured paints
- Paintbrushes and palettes
- Feathers
- Leaves
- Wildflowers
- Scissors
- An assortment of coloured wool
- Sticky tape
- Ribbons

What's in it for the children?

The children are able to forage for resources and design their own magical wand. The activity will require fine motor and attention skills to create the wand's handle.

Taking it forward

- Invite the children to create role play games around their magical wands.

- Use this activity alongside the potions laboratory activity (see page 16-17) to extend and offer further play opportunities.

What to do:

1. Ask each child to find a stick that they would like to use for their magical wand.

2. Invite the children to paint their sticks (if they want to), allowing them to choose and select whatever colours they would like to use.

3. Ensure that the paint has completely dried.

4. Encourage the children to explore the outdoor area to find feathers, leaves and wildflowers to attach to their magic wand.

5. Once they have found their natural embellishments, ask the children to use the scissors to cut a long piece of wool (roughly 60 cm).

6. Demonstrate to the children how they can create a handle on their magic wand by taking the piece of wool and tying it in a granny knot at the end of the stick, ensuring the tail of the wool is half the length of the stick.

7. Hold the tail of the string flat against the stick and begin to tightly wrap the rest of the string around the stick, once you have covered a quarter of the stick take the tail of the string and tie both ends in another knot.

8. Encourage the children to decorate their wands with their natural embellishments, using sticky tape, string and ribbons.

Natural picture frames

Supporting fine motor control

What you need:

- Four sticks of same width and length
- Ball of twine
- Scissors
- Leaves
- Grass
- Wildflowers
- Feathers
- Bark
- Natural embellishments

Top tip ⭐

This activity will need one-to-one support as the knots are tricky to start with.

What to do:

1. Ask the children to explore the area and find four sticks that are the same width and length.

2. Once they have found their sticks, ask them to place them on the ground in a square shape.

3. Invite each child to cut four long pieces of twine using scissors.

4. To create a frame, help the children to tie each point of the square together securely with the twine, using a clove hitch knot followed by a square lashing (a guide is available online at www.thechildcareguru.co.uk or you can watch a video tutorial at www.youtube.com/watch?v=9wpb9dELsa8).

5. Take the ball of twine and help the children to tie the loose end to a corner on the inside of the frame.

6. Encourage them to wrap the twine in the same direction around the frame. To keep this tight, loop twice around each end of the stick as you wrap.

7. Once the children have wrapped the twine around the frame in one direction, they now need to repeat this action in another direction pulling tight, so that they create small squares.

8. Invite the children to cut the string from the ball and tie a knot on the frame to secure the weave.

9. Now that the basis of the frame is ready, encourage the children to go foraging for their natural resources, e.g. leaves, grass, wildflowers, feathers, bark – anything they wish to use!

10. Demonstrate how to weave and thread the natural resources through the squares that they have created on their frame.

11. Allow the children to decorate as they wish, creating different patterns and exploring textures and colours.

What's in it for the children?

This is an opportunity for children to explore natural resources and use fine motor skills to tie knots and weave designs for their natural picture frames. They are also able to explore different colours, textures and patterns.

Taking it forward

- Create an outdoor art gallery, hanging up all of your natural picture frames.

Woodland broomsticks

Crafts to support imagination

What you need:

- Large stick
- Gardening gloves for children
- Scissors
- Long grass
- Bracken
- A ball of twine
- Ruler for measuring
- Ribbon
- Wool
- Paint

What to do:

1. Invite the children to forage for a large stick that they can use as a broomstick.

2. Once they have collected their stick, ask the children to use the scissors to cut some long grass or, wearing gardening gloves, to pick some bracken or any other suitable natural resources to act as the brush.

3. Show the children how to gather their grass or bracken into a bunch.

4. Using the ruler to measure 30 cm, ask the children to use the scissors to cut a piece of twine.

5. Using the twine, tie the grass or bracken around one end of the broomstick.

6. Allow the children to decorate and personalise their broomstick using any other materials that you may have, e.g. ribbons, wool and paint.

Top tip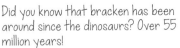

Did you know that bracken has been around since the dinosaurs? Over 55 million years!

What's in it for the children?

The children are able to forage for resources and design their own broomsticks which requires attention and fine and gross motor skills. Using scissors to cut grass is a great way to strengthen hand-eye coordination and fine motor control. Children also have the opportunity to learn about nature and all that grows around them while being aware of their surroundings and safety.

Taking it forward

- Introduce a story about witches and wizards to go alongside the play with broomsticks.

- Have broomstick races!

✚ Health & Safety

Ensure the children wear gardening gloves when picking bracken as it can cause splinters and friction burns.

Woodland wizards

Natural role play toys

What you need:

- One stick per child that is roughly the diameter of a 50p coin
- Gardening gloves for yourself and the children
- Small hacksaw
- A potato peeler
- Permanent markers
- Coloured wool
- Scissors
- Felt
- Super glue

What's in it for the children?

In this activity, children learn how to safely use tools and risk assess. They have to work on their listening and attention skills to follow the carefully-planned instructions, as well as strengthen their fine and gross motor control when using the tools and customising their wizards.

Taking it forward

- Build a home or school for the woodland wizards using sticks and natural resources.
- Create other characters using the same method.

✚ Health & Safety

Keep children well away from the super glue, ensuring that it is only used by adults. See page 5 for tips on safety when using tools.

What to do:

1. Show the children a thick stick that is roughly the diameter of a 50p coin (otherwise your woodland wizard will not stand up) and ask them to search for a stick that is the same size.

2. Ensure that you have a clear space around you and that there are no children close enough to get hurt. You should be 'two arms and a tool's length' away from any children.

3. Demonstrate how to safely use the hacksaw.

4. Wearing a gardening glove to protect yourself on your non-dominant hand, hold the stick. Place the stick over a log with the end hanging off (this is the part you wish to saw off).

5. Hold the hacksaw in your dominant hand and begin sawing slowly and steadily, backwards and forwards until the stick is cut.

6. Invite the children to wear gardening gloves and have a go, working with them one-to-one and explaining the safety procedures as you go.

7. Wearing a gardening glove on your non-dominant hand, demonstrate how to use a potato peeler to whittle away some of the stick (see page 24 for instructions). This will be the wizard's face.

8. Invite the children to pick a permanent marker and draw on their wizard's facial features.

9. Ask the children to cut several strips of coloured wool using scissors for the wizard's hair.

10. Help the children to cut a cone shape out of felt to make the wizard's hat.

11. Following the children's chosen design, attach the wizard's hair and hat to the wood securely with the super glue.

12. Encourage the children to use their wizard sticks during role play, small world play and with their peers.

Wizard's walking staff

Design and create a walking staff

What you need:

- A large stick
- Natural resources, e.g. pine cones, acorns, feathers
- Gardening gloves for yourself and the children
- A potato peeler
- An assortment of twine or string

What's in it for the children?

In this activity, children work on their fine motor, listening and attention skills when whittling. The children also have the opportunity to be creative when making and designing their own unique walking aid.

Taking it forward

- Use your staff while on a woodland walk.

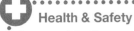
Health & Safety

See page 5 for tips on safety when using tools.

What to do:

1. Ask the children to explore the area and look for a large stick that will be their walking staff.

2. Once they have selected their large stick, invite them to search for natural resources that they may wish to use to decorate their staff, e.g. pine cones, acorns and feathers.

3. Wearing a gardening glove on your non-dominant hand, demonstrate how to use a potato peeler to whittle away some of the staff and create a pattern or to simply make it smoother to hold and touch (see page 24 for instructions).

4. Support the children in making a handle for the staff using twine or string. Tie a knot around the top of the staff, ensuring there is lots of twine or string left to wrap around the staff and for the tail.

5. Hold the tail of the twine flat against the staff for the child and ask them to begin to tightly wrap the other end of twine around the staff.

6. Encourage them to keep wrapping the twine until they get to the bottom of the tail of twine that you are holding against the staff. Use the tail to finish off the handle and tie a double knot to keep it secure.

7. Allow the children to decorate the staff by tying the natural resources they collected in step 2 to it.

Leaf printing

Exploring different leaves and their textures

What you need:

- Assortment of leaves
- Two pieces of paper for each child
- Tables or clipboards (optional)
- Paintbrushes for each child
- Different coloured paints

What to do:

1. Invite the children to explore and gather leaves of different shapes and sizes. Once they have at least five, they can begin their leaf printing.

2. Set up an area outside for painting – this could be on the ground or on tables or clipboards.

3. Demonstrate to the children how to print with their leaves. Place one of your pieces of paper onto a flat surface away from your leaves.

4. Next, place your leaves on another piece of paper, ensuring that it is on a flat surface.

5. Using a paintbrush, paint over a leaf. Make sure you go over the edges as this will create a print outline too.

6. Carefully pick up your painted leaf and place it paint-side down on your first sheet of paper that was kept away from the leaves. Use your fingertips to press it down so all the paint transfers.

7. Slowly lift up the leaf to reveal its print.

8. Allow the children to have a go, selecting different leaves and paints each time. They will have two different leaf print collages: the leaf's outline and the leaf itself.

9. Let the prints dry and then display for all to see.

What's in it for the children?

Children are able to explore different types of trees, leaves and textures when creating their leaf prints. This activity offers a messy play element as the children have to use paints and their hands to create the printings.

Taking it forward

- Take photographs of the trees that the leaves originally came from and match them up with your painted collage pictures.

Woodland mersticks
Natural role play toys

What you need:

- One stick per child that is roughly the diameter of a 50p coin
- Gardening gloves for yourself and the children
- Small hacksaw
- A potato peeler
- Permanent markers
- Coloured wool
- Scissors
- Felt
- Super glue

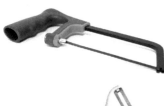

What to do:

1. Explain to the children that they are going to make a stick merperson – a 'merstick'. Show the children a thick stick that is roughly the diameter of a 50p coin and ask them to search for a stick that is the same size. Leave your stick out for them to compare.

2. Ensure that you have a clear space around you and that there are no children close enough to get hurt. You should be 'two arms and a tool's length' away from any children.

3. Demonstrate how to safely use the hacksaw: wearing a gardening glove to protect yourself on your non-dominant hand, hold the stick. Place the stick over a log with the end hanging off (this is the part you wish to saw off). Hold the hacksaw in your dominant hand and begin sawing slowly and steadily, backwards and forwards until the stick is cut.

4. Invite the children to wear gardening gloves and have a go, working with them one-to-one and explaining the safety procedures as you go.

5. Wearing a gardening glove on your non-dominant hand, demonstrate how to use a potato peeler to whittle away some of the stick (see page 24 for instructions). This will be the merstick's face.

6. Invite the children to pick a permanent marker and draw on their merstick's facial features.

7. Ask the children to cut several strips of coloured wool using scissors for the merstick's hair.

8. Help the children to cut a tail shape out of felt.

9. Following the children's chosen design, attach the merstick's hair and tail to the wood securely with the super glue.

10. Encourage the children to use their woodland merstick during role play, small world play and with their peers.

What's in it for the children?

In this activity, children learn how to safely use tools and risk assess. They have to work on their listening and attention skills to follow the carefully-planned instructions, as well as strengthen their fine and gross motor control when using the tools and customising their mersticks.

Taking it forward

- Use silk scarves to act like water for imaginative role play for the woodland mersticks.
- Create other characters using the same method.

➕ Health & Safety

Keep children well away from the super glue, ensuring that it is only used by adults. See page 5 for tips on safety when using tools.

Natural paintbrushes
Innovative ways to use nature

What you need:

- Feathers
- Branches
- Flowers
- Leaves
- Elder wood
- Hammer
- Gloves for yourself
- Paper for each child
- Paint and water

What's in it for the children?

The children are able to explore natural materials and see what prints and marks they can make with their natural paintbrushes. The activity also allows the children to compare their paintings and see which natural paintbrushes worked better than others and why.

Taking it forward

- Explore different materials to paint on outside, e.g. tree trunks.

Health & Safety

See page 5 for tips on safety when using tools.

What to do:

1. Invite the children to set up a painting station outside, on the ground or perhaps on a tree stump.

2. Ask the children to explore the area to gather different resources that will act as a paintbrush, e.g. feathers, branches, flowers and leaves.

3. Explore with the children to find some elder wood. You can break down the edge of the elder wood with a hammer to create a fan effect, which can then be used as a paintbrush. When using the hammer, wear a glove on your non-dominant hand. Ensure that you have a clear space around you and that there are no children close enough to get hurt. You should be 'two arms and a tool's length, away from any children.

4. Once the children have a selection of natural paintbrushes to use, let them begin to paint on their paper and explore the different patterns their paintbrushes create.

5. Encourage the children to paint pictures of their outdoor environment or what they can see.

6. Once finished, gather the children together to view each other's artwork. Discuss the different paintbrushes they used and what they decided to paint a picture of.

Natural bunting

Using natural resources to decorate outside

What you need:

- Strips of silver birch bark
- Scissors
- Eyelet plier
- Natural resources, e.g. pine cones and feathers
- A ball of twine

What to do:

1. Show the children what silver birch bark looks like and see if they can find any silver birch trees in the area.

2. Help the children to collect as many strips of silver birch bark as they can as this will act as shapes for the bunting. The bark will come away from fallen or dead trees easily.

3. Invite the children to cut large shapes out of the collected silver birch bark using scissors.

4. Explore the area again and ask the children to forage and collect more natural resources, such as pine cones and feathers.

5. Use the eyelet plier to create holes in the bark and natural resources so that string can be threaded through.

6. With the children, decide how long your bunting is going to be and ask them to hold out a piece of twine. When you have decided the length of the twine, cut it ready for threading.

7. Think about shape and pattern as the children come up with an order for the natural resources. Once they have decided on an order, lay the twine on the ground and place all the natural resources along it.

8. Help the children to thread or tie the resources onto the bunting using the twine.

9. Choose a place with the children to hang up the bunting and enjoy.

What's in it for the children?

Children are able to explore their natural environment while foraging for resources to create new crafts. This activity ignites conversations about the world around us and the shapes and patterns we can see.

Taking it forward

- Create other ways to use nature to decorate your outdoor areas, like natural dreamcatchers.

Natural outdoor mobile

Sensory play for little ones

What you need:

- Pieces of willow or long, bendy sticks
- A pair of secateurs
- Gardening gloves for yourself and the children
- Assortment of ribbons
- Natural resources, e.g. pine cones and feathers

Top tip

Willow needs to stay moist so water it regularly.

What's in it for the children?

This is an opportunity to explore natural materials in the outside environment. Children have to work together and use their communication and listening skills to make the mobiles. The older children are also helping to create and make mobiles for babies and toddlers which develops their understanding of the world and encourages them to care for others.

Taking it forward

- Create several archways in a line to create a tunnel or assault course.

What to do:

1. If you have willow growing in your outdoor area, demonstrate how to use the secateurs to cut pieces. Wear a gardening glove on your non-dominant hand and hold the tool in your dominant hand.

2. Allow the children to help, ensuring that they are also wearing gardening gloves.

3. If you do not have any willow, you can buy some from a local garden centre or find some in a public woodland. If willow is not available, you can use any long, bendy sticks that you can find.

4. Explore the outdoor area with the children and find a space that has soft ground.

5. Take the pieces of willow and, working in pairs, ask the children to bend them gently into an arch shape.

6. Help the children place both ends of the willow deep into the ground, creating an archway.

7. Explain to the children that they are going to tie ribbons and natural resources to the mobiles. Ask them to forage for natural resources like feathers and pine cones and bring them back to their archway.

8. Demonstrate how to attach a pine cone to a piece of ribbon and then loop it over the archway.

9. Repeat the process to create a mobile for younger babies and toddlers.

Cress heads

Grow your own cress

What you need:

- An egg for each child
- An apron for each child
- Small bowl
- Water
- Acrylic paints and paintbrushess
- Googly eyes (optional)
- Cotton wool
- Cress seeds

Top tip

A windowsill is a perfect place to put your cress head.

What to do:

1. Help each child to carefully remove the top of the egg with a spoon, leaving the bottom two-thirds of the eggshell intact.

2. Empty the egg from the shell into the bowl and rinse the shells with water. (Don't waste the eggs; cook them later.)

3. Invite the children to use paints to decorate their egg, adding facial features and googly eyes if you have them.

4. Let the painted eggshells dry fully.

5. Ask the children to dip small pieces of cotton wool in the bowl of water, squeezing out any excess.

6. Place the cotton wool at the bottom of the egg and, using the spoon, let the children add their cress seeds onto the cotton wool.

7. Place the 'cress heads' in a dry and well-lit place and watch the cress grow over time.

What's in it for the children?

The children are able to learn and understand about the process of growth from seeds, natural cycles and how to grow produce.

Taking it forward

- Once the cress has grown, cut some off and use to make egg and cress sandwiches.

Signs of spring adventures

Discover new life during spring

What you need:

- One camera per group

Top tip ⭐

A downloadable worksheet that the children can use to easily tick off their findings is available online at www.thechildcareguru.co.uk.

What to do:

1. Talk to children about the changing seasons and ask them if they know what happens during springtime.

2. Organise the children into small groups and explain that they are going to be looking for things that appear in spring outside.

3. Help the groups look for signs of spring, e.g. butterflies, daffodils, frogspawn, blossom, dandelions and bluebells. They will need to look all around them when they are on their adventure – up in the sky and down on the ground.

4. Ask the children to look for buds on trees and fresh new leaves. Can they compare their sizes?

5. Encourage the children to take pictures using the camera of any signs of spring they come across.

6. Bring the groups together and ask the children to share their findings. What have they learnt about spring?

Signs of Spring Adventure

@The Childcare Guru

Butterflies ☐

Daffodils ☐

Frogs Spawn ☐

Can you find any buds on the trees or fresh new leaves too?

Blossom ☐

Dandelions ☐

Bluebells ☐

Can you find these signs of Spring?

What's in it for the children?

This idea enables children to learn about the changing seasons, supporting their understanding about the world and our environment. It is a great opportunity to start conversations about cycles and new life as the children observe buds growing and flowers. The activity also focuses on attention and visual skills as children go on their adventure to search for signs of spring.

Taking it forward

- Introduce life cycles to the children by showing how new life begins during springtime, e.g. the life cycle of a frog.

- Make a photo collage for each season.

Signs of summer adventures

There's so much to see in summer!

Top tip ⭐

A downloadable worksheet that the children can use to easily tick off their findings is available online at www.thechildcareguru.co.uk.

What's in it for the children?

This is an opportunity for children to learn about the seasons and the changes that occur around us, supporting their understanding about the world and our environment. The activity focuses on attention and visual skills as children go on their adventure to search for signs of summer. Children are also able to develop their mathematical language as they count and compare sizes.

Taking it forward

- Print photographs and compare the findings each season to see and compare the differences and changes that occur, e.g. the colours found in summer versus those found in winter.

- Collect samples of the different colours the children find to create a summer collage.

What to do:

1. Talk to children about the changing seasons and ask them if they know what happens during summertime.

2. Place the children into small groups and explain that they are going to be looking for things that appear in summer outside.

3. Help the groups look for signs of summer, e.g. bees, bramble, ladybirds, foxglove, dragonflies and dog roses. They will need to look all around them when they are on their adventure – up in the sky and down on the ground.

4. Ask the children to count the number of spots they can see on a ladybird and to look for fledglings learning to fly. Can they compare their sizes?

5. Encourage the children to take pictures using the camera of any signs of summer they come across.

6. Bring the groups together and ask the children to share their findings. What have they learnt about summer?

Signs of autumn adventures

Explore the changes through autumn

What you need:

- One camera per group

Top tip ★

A downloadable worksheet that the children can use to easily tick off their findings is available online at www.thechildcareguru.co.uk.

What's in it for the children?

The activity encourages children to learn about the seasons and the changes that occur around us, supporting their understanding about the world and our environment. The activity focuses on attention and visual skills as children go on an adventure to search for signs of autumn.

Taking it forward

- Print photographs and compare the findings each season, so children clearly see and compare the differences and changes that occur.
- Create leaf art using coloured leaves.

✚ Health & Safety

Fungi like the fly agaric mushroom (shown right) can be poisonous. Ensure the children are careful when observing the fungi and do not touch them.

What to do:

1. Talk to children about the changing seasons and ask them if they know what happens during autumn.

2. Place the children into small groups and explain that they are going to be looking for things that appear in autumn outside.

3. Help the groups look for signs of autumn, e.g. red, orange and yellow leaves, conkers, grey squirrels and fungi. They will need to look all around them when they are on their adventure – up in the sky and down on the ground.

4. Encourage the children to take pictures using the camera of any signs of autumn they come across.

5. Bring the groups together and ask the children to share their findings. What have they learnt about autumn?

Signs of winter adventures

What will you find this winter?

What you need:

- One camera per group

Top tip ⭐

A downloadable worksheet that the children can use to easily tick off their findings is available online at www.thechildcareguru.co.uk.

What to do:

1. Talk to children about the changing seasons and ask them if they know what happens during winter.

2. Place the children into small groups and explain that they are going to be looking for things that appear in winter outside.

3. Help the groups look for signs of winter, e.g. holly, frost, bird nests, catkins, moss and pine cones. They will need to look all around them when they are on their adventure – up in the sky and down on the ground.

4. Ask the children if they can spot any bird nests in the bare trees.

5. Encourage the children to take pictures using the camera of any signs of winter they come across.

6. Bring the groups together and ask the children to share their findings. What have they learnt about winter?

What's in it for the children?

Children are able to learn about the seasons and the changes that occur around us, supporting their understanding about the world and our environment. The activity focuses on attention and visual skills as children explore outside to find signs of winter.

Taking it forward

- Collect pine cones for craft activities, e.g. to create a pine cone hedgehog or a Christmas decoration.

- Make a photo collage for each season.

Leaf threading

Developing fine motor control

What you need:

- One small, thin stick for each child
- Gardening gloves for yourself and the children
- Potato peeler
- Scissors
- String
- Assortment of leaves

What's in it for the children?

This activity helps the children to develop their fine motor control when threading the leaves.

Taking it forward

- Create different patterns with the leaves, using sequences and colours.
- Ask the children to count how many leaves they have threaded to develop their mathematical understanding.

➕ **Health & Safety**

See page 5 for tips on safety when using tools.

What to do:

1. Ask the children to forage for small, thin sticks.

2. Wearing a gardening glove on your non-dominant hand, demonstrate how to use a potato peeler to whittle down the end of the stick to create a point (see page 24 for instructions).

3. Do this with the children one-to-one in order to keep everyone safe. Let them use the peeler if appropriate, and ensure that they wear gardening gloves.

4. Using scissors, cut long pieces of string for each child. Demonstrate how to double knot the string to the end of the stick without the pointed end.

5. Invite the children to explore the area and to collect leaves of different shapes, colours and sizes.

6. The children can use the pointed part of the stick as a 'needle' to create holes in the leaves. They can then begin to thread the leaves onto the string.

7. Once all of the leaves have been threaded, help the children to tie a double knot at the end of the string.

Bark rubbings

Learning about the differences in trees

What you need:

- **Three squares of paper for each child**
- **Coloured crayons**
- **Camera**

Top tip ⭐

When creating the rubbings, make sure the crayon or chalk is placed on its side otherwise the paper will tear.

What to do:

1. Note the types of trees in the outside area.

2. Give each child three small squares of paper and a coloured crayon of their choice.

3. Ask the children to find a tree to make a bark rubbing.

4. Explain that to make a bark rubbing, the children have to place a piece of paper over the bark. Holding the crayon flat, they need to rub it across the paper. This will create a pattern from the bark of that tree.

5. Encourage the children to make bark rubbings on different trees using their other two squares of paper.

6. Compare the textures and patterns of the bark from the different types of trees. Can the children name the types of trees?

7. Take photographs of the trees that the children used to make the bark rubbings. Can the children match the bark rubbings to the correct tree?

What's in it for the children?

Children are able to learn about different trees and their names. This activity is also an opportunity to explore textures and patterns and discuss their differences.

Taking it forward

- Add the bark rubbings and the photographs of the trees they came from to a natural art scrapbook to create a tree reference book for your classroom.

Bird nests

Building homes to protect our wildlife

What you need:

- Bendy twigs
- Sticks
- Leaves
- Stones
- Flowers
- Moss

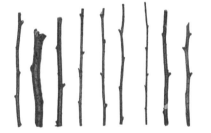

What to do:

1. Talk to the children about different types of birds they might see in the outdoor area, inviting them to talk about any birds they have seen flying around.

2. In groups, ask the children to create a bird nest for their favourite bird.

3. Encourage the children to forage in the area and collect the resources they need to build their nests, e.g. bendy twigs, sticks, leaves, stones and flowers. They do not have to collect it all at once; they will figure out what they need as they go along.

4. Help the children create the foundations of the nest with bendy twigs and sticks.

5. Encourage conversations about how to keep the birds warm and safe, e.g. with moss. What resources might the children use?

6. Let the children be creative in how they decide to decorate their nest.

7. Once all the nests have been built, allow the children to take it in turns to talk about their unique nest and what bird they made it for.

What's in it for the children?

This activity enhances children's knowledge and understanding about different types of birds and their habitats. Children are able to connect with nature and the environment, while developing their teamwork skills and the communication of ideas and thoughts.

Taking it forward

- Make one giant bird nest so that the children can pretend to be the birds.

Cosy bug hotels

Creating eco-systems

What you need:

- Moss
- Leaves
- Bark
- Pine cones
- Soil
- Stones
- Sticks
- Wooden crates
- Bricks with holes
- Wooden planks
- Old tiles
- Old piece of wood
- Permanent markers

What to do:

1. Discuss with the children how to design a bug hotel and what materials will be needed to build it.

2. Ask the children to look for and collect natural resources for the hotel, e.g. moss, leaves, bark, pine cones, soil, stones and sticks.

3. Help the children build their bug hotel from the ground upwards, starting with a wooden crate as the base.

4. Let the children take it in turns to continue to build the hotel, adding bricks, more crates, wooden planks, bark and soil. Can they create different crevices and places for bugs to hide?

5. Spark the children's imaginations by suggesting different uses for the natural materials, e.g. moss could be a soft comfy carpet for the bugs and leaves could be blankets. Let the children be creative with their ideas.

6. Once the children have built the bug hotel, they will need to create a roof to keep it fairly dry. Invite the children to create a waterproof roof – moss and old tiles work perfectly.

7. Ask the children to personalise the bug hotel by making a sign to go outside using an old piece of wood and permanent markers.

8. Observe the bug hotel to see which bugs and insects visit.

What's in it for the children?

The children have the opportunity to learn about the ecosystem and the many types of insects and bugs. As well as constructing and designing the bug hotel, the children will have to work together as a team and communicate and share ideas.

Taking it forward

- Count how many different insect species visit the bug hotel.

Colour matching
Supporting colour recognition

What you need:
- Colour wheel or cards
- Camera

Top tip ⭐

DIY stores are great for collecting sample colour wheels or cards as they sell many paint colours.

What's in it for the children?

This activity helps children recognise and name different colours as well as compare shades of colours. Children are able to explore their environment and discover new natural resources that they can ask questions about to further their knowledge and understanding. This activity will differ depending on the season, which opens discussions about changes during seasons and the colours that appear.

Taking it forward

- Carry out this activity during each of the four seasons, taking photographs and making comparisons about the changes.

✚ Health & Safety

Ensure that you are aware of any poisonous plants in the area and do not allow children to pick or touch plants that are unsafe.

What to do:

1. Give each child a colour card, tailored to the season and colours that are likely to be found.

2. Ask the children to explore outdoors and see if they can find any natural resources that match the different colours on the cards they have.

3. Encourage the children to identify the colours by name.

4. When the children find a match, take a photograph of the colour card and the resource together so that you can compare everyone's findings later.

5. Once the children have matched as many cards as they can, print out the pictures taken.

6. Reflect upon the findings: which colours were found easily? Which colours were not found?. Encourage an open group discussion between the children, e.g. 'Why do you think you didn't find that colour?'.

Bird feeders
Caring for our wildlife

What you need:

- Large bag of wild birdseed
- Cups
- Lard or vegetable fat
- A bowl for each group
- Half of a coconut shell for each group
- Gardening gloves for yourself and each child
- Scissors
- Twine
- Non-electric hand drill

Top tip

Give the children gloves to wear while handling the birdseed and lard mixture if they are uncomfortable touching the texture.

What to do:

1. Organise the children into small groups.
2. Invite the children to empty two cups of birdseed into the bowl.
3. Next, give each group a piece of lard to add to their bowls.
4. Ask the children to use their hands to mix together the birdseed and lard until the mixture is all stuck together. The children may need to add more lard at this stage if it is not all sticking together.
5. Give each group half a coconut shell.
6. The children should wear a gardening glove on their non-dominant hand. On a flat surface like a tree stump, support the children in using a hand drill to create a small hole in the top of the coconut shell.
7. Invite the children to cut a piece of twine about 20 cm long using scissors and to fold it in half to make a loop.
8. Show the children how to thread the loop through the hole in the coconut. Tie a knot using the two ends of the string once the loop is three-quarters of the way through the coconut. This will allow the children to hang their bird feeder from a tree branch.
9. Using their hands, ask the children to fill their coconut half with the birdseed and lard mixture, pressing it all firmly in.
10. Find somewhere in the outdoor area to hang the bird feeders.
11. Make sure the children wash their hands with lots of soap as lard is water resistant.

What's in it for the children?

The children are able to learn about caring for the local wildlife. Making the bird feeders is a hands-on sensory activity where the children can explore the feel and texture of the birdseed and lard mixture.

Taking it forward

- Take photographs of the birds enjoying their new feeders.

- Find out the names of all the birds that have eaten from the bird feeders.

 **Health & Safety**
See page 5 for tips on safety when using tools.

Animal habitats

Understanding wildlife

What you need:

- Sticks
- Moss
- Leaves
- Stones
- Twigs
- Bark

Top tip ⭐

This activity can be done in groups to support teamwork and communication.

What's in it for the children?

This activity will develop the children's understanding of wildlife and their habitats. It will build upon their reflection and communication skills and encourage self-confidence as they describe their constructions.

Taking it forward

- Compare the habitats the children have made with images of real animal homes.

What to do:

1. Have an open discussion with the children about habitats, asking them what they think a habitat is. Support the children's knowledge and understanding on the topic and answer any questions they may have.

2. Discuss the different types of woodland animals and birds that the children might find in the UK.

3. Ask them to pick their favourite woodland animal. Explain that they are going to build a cosy habitat for the woodland animal to live in.

4. Encourage the children to forage for natural resources that can be used to create a habitat, e.g. sticks, moss, leaves, stones, twigs and bark.

5. Help the children to create a habitat using the natural resources gathered. Can they build a habitat that will keep the animal safe, dry and warm?

6. As a group, observe and compare the constructed habitats for the woodland animals.

7. Invite the children to describe what they have designed, how they built the habitat and what materials they used. Did they add any special features for their chosen woodland animal?

Tracking game

Supporting gross motor skills and senses

What you need:

- Sticks
- Leaves
- Stones
- Pine cones

What to do:

1. Divide the children into two groups and assign an adult to each one.

2. As the first group heads off into the outdoor area, the second group must wait at least ten minutes before following. Sing songs or play a game with the children as you wait.

3. The first group need to leave a trail behind for the second group to follow. Encourage the children to make arrows out of sticks, leaves and stones, placing them on the ground to tell the second group which direction to go in.

4. Help the children make 'X' signs out of natural resources to show the second group which way not to go. The children can also leave other markers on the ground to give hints, e.g. pine cones.

5. Once the first group have created their trail of hints, they must hide near the last clue.

6. The second group must now follow the trail using the clues left behind. Can they find the first group?

What's in it for the children?

The children must use teamwork and social communication to successfully leave a trail and work out the clues. Those in the second group will also need to use navigation and sensory skills in order to find the first group.

Taking it forward

- The children can use a compass to work out whether the first group went north, south, east or west.

Scavenger hunt

Exploring the outdoors

What you need:

- Scissors
- Cardboard for each child
- Double-sided sticky tape
- Natural resources
- Fungi
- Flowers
- Berries
- Leaves

What's in it for the children?

A scavenger hunt offers the children the opportunity to discover nature and what they might find at different times of the year. Children can compare and discuss their findings while learning about different plants and trees.

Taking it forward

- Create a giant collage of all of the natural resources found, take a picture and add it to a nature scrapbook.

➕ Health & Safety

Always carry a first aid kit with you when on a scavenger hunt and have water available. Remind the children that they should never eat anything they find on a scavenger hunt.

What to do:

1. Supervise the children as they cut shapes out of the cardboard using scissors. The cardboard shapes should be no bigger than an A5 piece of paper but still large enough to collect resources on.

2. Help the children attach double-sided sticky tape onto the cardboard, leaving out one edge that they can use to hold the board.

3. Take the children outside on a nature scavenger hunt to see what they can find.

4. The children can collect items to stick onto their cardboard as they go, although they should check that it is safe to pick up the natural resource first, e.g. fungi, flowers and berries.

5. As a group, discuss what was found during the scavenger hunt, e.g. what colours did they find? What textures and patterns do the natural resources have? What tree did the leaves come from?

6. Support each child to voice their opinions and thoughts openly if they want to.

Clay printing

Experimenting with textures and prints

What you need:

- Natural resources, e.g. leaves, feathers, wildflowers
- Air-drying clay
- Watercolour paints and paintbrushes

Top tip

Make sure you seal up the leftover clay and keep in an airtight container to prevent it drying out.

What's in it for the children?

Natural art enables children to be creative and develop their fine motor skills as they carefully handle the natural resources. Children can explore textures and patterns while learning about different leaves, trees and plants.

Taking it forward

- Create a nature table to display your clay prints and showcase pictures of the natural resources that were used.

What to do:

1. Explore the outdoor area and ask the children to collect a variety of natural resources, e.g. leaves, feathers and wildflowers that they would like to use to make a print. Encourage them to choose resources that are different textures and sizes.

2. Talk to the children about the resources they have collected. Can they name the trees that the leaves belong to? What is the flower called?

3. Let each child tear off a piece of the air-drying clay and split it into two or three pieces.

4. Demonstrate how to flatten out the clay using your hands. This can be done on a tree stump, table or the ground.

5. Once the children have flattened a piece of clay, they can press their first natural resource into the clay using their fingertips and count to ten before carefully removing it. This will leave an imprint of the natural resource in the clay.

6. The children can repeat this process with their other pieces of clay to create clay discs with different imprints.

7. Leave the clay in the sunshine to dry or indoors in a warm place.

8. Once the clay is dry, invite the children to paint their imprinted clay discs using watercolour paints which will make the patterns stand out.

9. Use the painted discs as decorations or ornaments to display.

Hapa zome
Wildflower and leaf bashing

What you need:

- Selection of wildflowers
- Leaves
- White cloth squares
- Hammer
- Gardening gloves for yourself and the children

Top tip

- Pillowcases or sheets are ideal for making squares of white cloth.
- This activity works best when the wildflowers and leaves have moisture in them.

What to do:

1. Explain to the children that they will be doing an activity called 'hapa zome' which is a Japanese term that means 'leaf dye'. They will be bashing wildflowers and leaves to dye a cloth.

2. Let the children forage outside for wildflowers and leaves, or alternatively use flowers that are coming to the end of their shelf life.

3. Talk to the children about the different flowers they have chosen. Can they name the flowers?

4. Give each child a piece of white cloth.

5. Ask the children to put the cloth on a flat work surface, e.g. a tree stump, a table or the floor, and place their chosen flowers and leaves on one half of the cloth. They should then fold the cloth in half.

6. Demonstrate to the children how to carefully use a hammer.

7. When using the hammer, wear a glove on your non-dominant hand. Ensure that you have a clear space around you and that there are no children close enough to get hurt. You should be 'two arms and a tool's length' away from any children.

8. Hold the hammer in your dominant hand and tap over the cloth, squashing the flowers and leaves as you go. The colours will begin to imprint on the cloth.

9. Invite the children to wear gardening gloves and have a go, working with them one-to-one and explaining the safety procedures as you go.

10. Encourage the children to keep going until they have tapped over the entire cloth. They should take their time and watch what they are doing at all times.

11. Once the children have finished tapping the cloth, let them open it up to see the imprint of the flowers and leaves on both sides of the cloth.

12. Hang the cloths up to dry and then display when fully dry.

What's in it for the children?

This activity is an opportunity for children to learn about different flowers and how to imprint on to cloth. The children also gain an understanding of how to use tools and create art with nature.

Taking it forward

- Create prints throughout the seasons to compare and contrast the colours and resources available.

✚ Health & Safety

Ensure that you are aware of any poisonous plants in the area and do not allow children to pick or touch plants that are unsafe. See page 5 for tips on safety when using tools.

Animal tracking

Recognising animal prints and markings

What you need:

- Piece of paper and clipboard for each child
- Pencil for each child
- Camera
- Scrapbook

What's in it for the children?

The children are able to understand and learn about nature and animals. This activity encourages children to make links and learn about wildlife, their patterns of behaviour and habitats. The children have to tune in with their visual abilities to look out for animal tracks and follow any leads.

Taking it forward

- Create profiles about the animals that the children find tracks for and learn more about their habitats.

✚ Health & Safety

Remind the children that they should never touch animal faeces or habitats. If they come across any wild animals, they should keep a safe distance and not try to touch them, keeping quiet and calm at all times.

What to do:

1. Explain to the children that you are going on an adventure to look for animal tracks.

2. Ask the children what they think they may find, allowing them to take turns to share their ideas. Describe what different animal tracks they may find.

3. Take the children outside and encourage them to search the ground for paw prints, animal faeces and track patterns.

4. Give each child a piece of paper attached to a clipboard and a pencil and invite them to draw pictures of the tracks they find. Can the children identify which animal the tracks belong to?

5. Take photographs of any evidence the children find and follow the trails to see where they might lead. Can the children find the animal's habitat?

6. Print out the photographs and place them into a scrapbook to document and compare what the children find each time they go animal tracking. Do the children notice any patterns and changes in the findings at different times of the day and year?

Sound hide

Supporting rhythm and listening skills

What you need:

- An outdoor space with places to hide
- Sticks
- A log or tree

What's in it for the children?

This game encourages the children to use their senses as they try to sneak up on the sound maker. They must use auditory and gross motor skills to navigate and move quickly and quietly.

Taking it forward

- Make the game more complicated by asking the children to hide when the sound maker stops. If the sound maker sees any children when the rhythm is stopped, those children are out and must sit down.

What to do:

1. Gather the children outside together and explain the rules of the game, demonstrating how it works.

2. Pick one child to be the sound maker and ask them to sit with their back to all of the other children.

3. Ask the other children to find a hiding space.

4. The sound maker needs to tap out a rhythm using sticks against a log or a tree.

5. While the rhythm is being played, all the other children leave their hiding place and try to edge closer to the sound maker.

6. When the sound maker stops the rhythm, everyone else must stop moving.

7. The sound maker needs to turn around and see if they can spot anyone moving. If they can, the child moving is out and must sit down.

8. Encourage the sound maker to keep starting and stopping the rhythm until one person taps them on the shoulder.

Ice flowers
Sensory play

What you need:

- Assortment of wildflowers
- Scissors to share
- Container for each child
- Jugs of cold water
- Freezer
- Trays

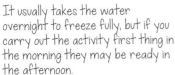

Top tip ⭐

It usually takes the water overnight to freeze fully, but if you carry out the activity first thing in the morning they may be ready in the afternoon.

What to do:

1. Let the children forage outside for wildflowers. Alternatively, you can use cut flowers that are coming to the end of their life.

2. Talk to the children about the flowers that they have chosen focusing on colours and the sounds heard in the names of the flowers. Can the children name the flowers themselves?

3. Using scissors if needed, ask the children to carefully remove the flower heads from the stems. Remind the children that if they touch the flowers petals too much they will wilt.

4. Ask the children to place the flower heads into a container, filling it halfway.

5. Invite the children to pour cold water from the jugs to fill up the container. The flowers will pop up when the water is poured in, so tell the children to gently push them down so they are submerged in the water.

6. Help the children to carefully place their containers in the freezer.

7. Once the water is completely frozen, remove the containers from the freezer and place them on a table or tray. Empty the ice out of their containers.

8. The children will be able to see the wildflowers through the ice. Encourage them to identify the wildflowers.

9. Let the children explore the ice and flowers through sensory play.

What's in it for the children?

This activity leads to sensory play which allows children to build up nerve connections within the brain's neural pathways, supporting learning. Using wildflowers also builds upon their knowledge about nature and invites talk about colours, textures and patterns.

Taking it forward

- Create a role play kitchen activity using the ice flowers as props.

- Freeze different items in the containers, perhaps conkers, acorns or feathers.

✚ Health & Safety

Ensure that you are aware of any poisonous plants in the area and do not allow children to pick or touch plants that are unsafe. Some flowers are poisonous when ingested, so make sure that the children do not put the ice or flowers in their mouths.

One, two, three, where are you?

Encouraging the use of senses

What you need:

- An outdoor area with places to hide

What's in it for the children?

This game encourages children to rely on their auditory sense, as they have to use sound and hearing to find their peers. The children also have to communicate and work together as a team to find those hiding, use their gross motor skills to navigate around the outdoor area and remain quiet when hiding.

Taking it forward

- Evolve the game to include other senses, e.g. use blindfolds to eliminate the counter's sight so they have to focus even more on their auditory senses.

✚ Health & Safety

Create a boundary so the children know how far away they can hide. You could tie ribbons around trees as indicators.

What to do:

1. Gather the children outside together and explain the rules of the game, demonstrating how it works.

2. Choose one child to be the counter. They must close their eyes and count out loud to ten slowly.

3. Help the other children find a hiding place.

4. Once the counter reaches ten, they should call out in their loudest voice, 'One, two, three, where are you?'.

5. The children that are hiding must remain hidden but reply loudly, 'One, two, three,, I am over here!'.

6. The counter must listen and follow the sound of the voices to discover where the other children are hiding. They can repeat the question, 'One, two, three, where are you?' as many times as they would like. Those hiding must always reply.

7. When the counter finds a child hiding, that child must join the hunt to find everyone else, helping the counter to ask the question, 'One, two, three, where are you?'.

8. This is repeated until there is only one child hiding. This child becomes the next counter.